DOMINI LEONARD

love, bring myself

Broken Sleep Books
brokensleepbooks.com

Published 2019,
Broken Sleep Books:
Carmarthenshire, Wales

brokensleepbooks.com

First Edition

Lay out your unrest.

Publisher/Editor: Aaron Kent
Editor: Charlie Baylis

Typeset in UK by Aaron Kent

Broken Sleep Books is committed to
a sustainable future for our planet,
and therefore uses print on
demand publication.

brokensleepbooks@gmail.com

ISBN: 9781795642699

Contents

love, bring myself

†

Here undernethe Me nowe a nexile I neven,
Whilke ile sall be Erthe

do you think these words…?   can you hear?
   (has) happened, say anything?   Whose is it?
   Who is there?   what I tell him is true?   What
more kindness…?   Is this…?   Why?   mean?

   do you hear?   dear, who else?   do you
believe (that) he is…?   moon?   do you hurry…?
   are you just guessing?   can you do that?
   What is your name?   are you trying to put it

into verse?   have you finished?   (who) is made
on earth   Why do you call him…?   What are
you doing?   are these things true…?   I think

that it means…   What do you think (now)?
   Where do you want to be?   which of us…?
   meet, where?   gone?   Ah, love, are you here?

this hour (i.e. now)   carries everything away   As
a sign   star   in sight   intended   Broke in
two   moor   pasture   circle, moon   next to you
(i.e. never in the same place)   we (go)   an owl

on a stump   path, street   (this) place (i.e. on earth)
    It seems to me   hum, hum, definitely   If you
will listen   With what shall they…   homewards
    bound   From which…for ever   I wish this

    Unless you tell the truth   healed me completely
    bushes, house, build   astonished, not move   I
swear (it)   know   stone   eyes, opened   at once

    in no place   very dark   Away, all (fall)   If,
comes in any way   dark   an anchorite's cell
    (that) is made for you   This much I know

(Even) if, go without   Completely   whilst   I
hate   [I] may not easily step over two straws
     shape, beauty, fixed   done   until   are   I'm
out of breath   (That there is not)   unworthy

of clothes (i.e. wicked)   would be   Our bodies
stun me with horror   Who have any need   Ah,
who   I carried one among the others   It's all
going wrong   I am ashamed of my body   As

I stand here   Forever, truly   leave, while it is
light   leaf   bliss   lost   Having wandered
     4,600 years   I am happy I lived long enough

     endless (i.e. everlasting)   sky   know, those
were his words   Other than, no one   Now go
     I don't know what's best   where we are heading

woods, in a light, made   bones, as lead   With
    (go on)   breathe, it is clear to see   eyes
    crying   might mean   risk/(cause of) anger
    stop   do not judge us for that   I suffer my

pain   thought nothing of it   breastbone, singing,
bored   it's nearly midnight   moon, ended
    if only it was…   where (there) is   happiness
    do not hold back   hold (i.e. keep)   Unending

    (i.e. all the time)   I do not need to worry at all
    isle   there is nothing else like it   hold out
your hand   undress yourself   But (must)   my

entire heart   fear   I must carry it to Bethlehem
    (my) skin, whatever caused it   what do you want
me to do to you   release from (Job 10:21)   Where

Hear   directly at   If, (from) where   dead, road
    less   safety   gather   in no place   according
to   What   wisdom   afraid   darkness   dogs
    eel   listen   in   once   knows   (to) find

out   don't waste your breath   depart, bliss   like
(a)   Thus come the   hill   'seas'   fair   (Even)
though   this house   we need no further evidence
    laid (down)   openly   merely empty   (i.e. until

you die)   nothing, about it   mirror/reflection
    quiet   then   support   on   Allow   truth
    tree   divinity   Whoever, matter   look here!

    harm, we need never fear   this weather is, clothed
    moon, stars   (anything) other than one   (You)
would make me   heartfelt   spoken   see (i.e. hear)

before you go   there   believe (that) you were there
     for a time   for this reason   for no other reason
     touch him   I do not know how   no one   may
     Openly   great (place of) bliss   It, alone   (go

in) procession   completely and openly   enough
has been said   Unless, can, signs   in fellowship
(i.e. together)   No one else came   no one,
but us   faces at the moon   each one   love,

bring myself   loved one   false, I see that you are
     dumb, door, did, remain   do you deny   What
it means   revealed   'the earth'   brightness

     you know nothing   you can be sure of that
     not worry   From, if I know where   save
(i.e. keep) them   farewell   completely, at once

endless (i.e. everlasting)   For   there is no beginning
    veins   moors   good advice   These, are beyond
me   'Had I known…' is no good   waning (of the
moon)   How   complete   flower of most beautiful

colour   It's a miracle! (ironic)   I will (into being), one
    If at any time…   gathered by arrangement   as
wretches, indeed   Sir, we'd like to know   palms,
flowers, harmony   (in just the right position)   from

nothing   If I thought you would hear me   outside,
weary, wet   (ever)lasting   what does it mean
    sun and moon   evening   Whatever happens

    Not until   until I've seen him   I have been trying
to (be)   wholly   radiant   beautiful   baffled   Even
if   (I will) turn (them away)   you shall always find me

To all I sall wirke be ʒhe wysshyng

Notes

The text of these poems is lifted from the glosses and translations of the 14th and 15th-century Corpus Christi plays as found in Greg Walker's edition, *Medieval Drama: An Anthology* (Blackwell, 2000). Walker: 'Medieval drama took many forms, but the most spectacular of all was the civic religious drama of towns such as York, Chester, Coventry, and Wakefield, referred to most commonly in modern times as the Mystery Plays or the Corpus Christi plays. For perhaps three hundred years before the building of the London playhouses, these plays held sway as the most popular and enduring form of drama in England, and were performed annually – or at least in most years – in many of the largest towns and cities in the country.'

The quotations on pages 7 and 23 are lines spoken by God in the first York play, *The Fall of the Angels* (ll. 27-28, l. 159).

Acknowledgements

Thank you: Camille, Tom, Sarah Annabel, Aaron, Prof. Bose, and Prof. Walker, for contributions major and minor.

This book is dedicated to Mary Anne Clark.

LAY OUT YOUR UNREST

Printed in Great Britain
by Amazon

60604357R00020